Meet NASA Inventor Robert Youngquist and His

Solar-Surfing Space Probes

WORLD BOOK

www.worldbook.com

World Book, Inc.
180 North LaSalle Street
Suite 900
Chicago, Illinois 60601
USA

For information about other World Book publications, visit our website at www.worldbook.com or call 1-800-WORLDBK (967-5325).

For information about sales to schools and libraries, call 1-800-975-3250 (United States), or 1-800-837-5365 (Canada).

Produced in collaboration with the National Aeronautics and Space Administration (NASA).

Library of Congress Cataloging-in-Publication Data for this volume has been applied for.

Out of This World
ISBN: 978-0-7166-6261-7 (set, hc.)

Solar-Surfing Space Probes
ISBN: 978-0-7166-6262-4 (hc.)
ISBN: 978-0-7166-6278-5 (pf.)

Also available as:
ISBN: 978-0-7166-6270-9 (e-book)

Staff

Editorial

Director
Tom Evans

Manager, New Content
Jeff De La Rosa

Writer
William D. Adams

Proofreader/Indexer
Nathalie Strassheim

Graphics and Design

Senior Visual
Communications Designer
Melanie Bender

Media Researcher
Rosalia Bledsoe

Acknowledgments

Cover   © Skorzewiak/Shutterstock; © Elenarts/Shutterstock
4-11   © Shutterstock
12-13   NASA/SDO
14   Bob Youngquist
16-21   © Shutterstock
23-31   NASA
33-35   Bob Youngquist
36-37   NASA/SDO
38-41   © Shutterstock
42-43   NASA/Steele Hill
44   Bob Youngquist

Contents

Glossary There is a glossary of terms on page 45. Terms defined in the glossary are in boldface type that **looks like this** on their first appearance on any spread (two facing pages).

Pronunciations (how to say words) are given in parentheses the first time some difficult words appear in the book. They look like this: pronunciation (pruh NUHN see AY shuhn).

Introduction

Since perhaps ancient times, people have dreamed of exploring the distant stars. But the most important star may be the one closest to home. The sun is the star at the center of our **solar system.** Earth and all the other familiar planets revolve around it. Energy from the sun warms our world, lights our days, and enables plants and other living things to make food.

It is natural to want to learn more about such an important part of our lives. But though the sun is nearby, studying it presents some serious challenges. One of the most important is heat. The heart of the sun is a massive nuclear reactor. There, atomic *nuclei* (cores) of the element hydrogen are combined to form nuclei of the element helium. This reaction churns out huge amounts of energy, which are flung into space in the form of **radiation.** It is this radiation that warms our planet, making it possible for life as we know it. But that same energy would fry a spacecraft at close range.

In 2018, the National Aeronautics and Space Administration (NASA) launched the Parker Solar Probe. This robotic spacecraft was built to study the sun more closely than ever before. Its design featured a state-of-the-art heat shield to protect the craft from the sun's searing temperatures. Yet the **probe's** closest approach was targeted for 4 million miles (6 million kilometers) above the solar surface.

To unlock all the secrets of our home star, future probes will have to get closer than that. To do so, they will need serious protection. The NASA inventor and physicist Bob Youngquist is working to develop a heat-resistant coating that could help future probes practically surf the solar surface. In doing so, he may also revolutionize the way spacecraft fuel up, speed up, and protect their crew.

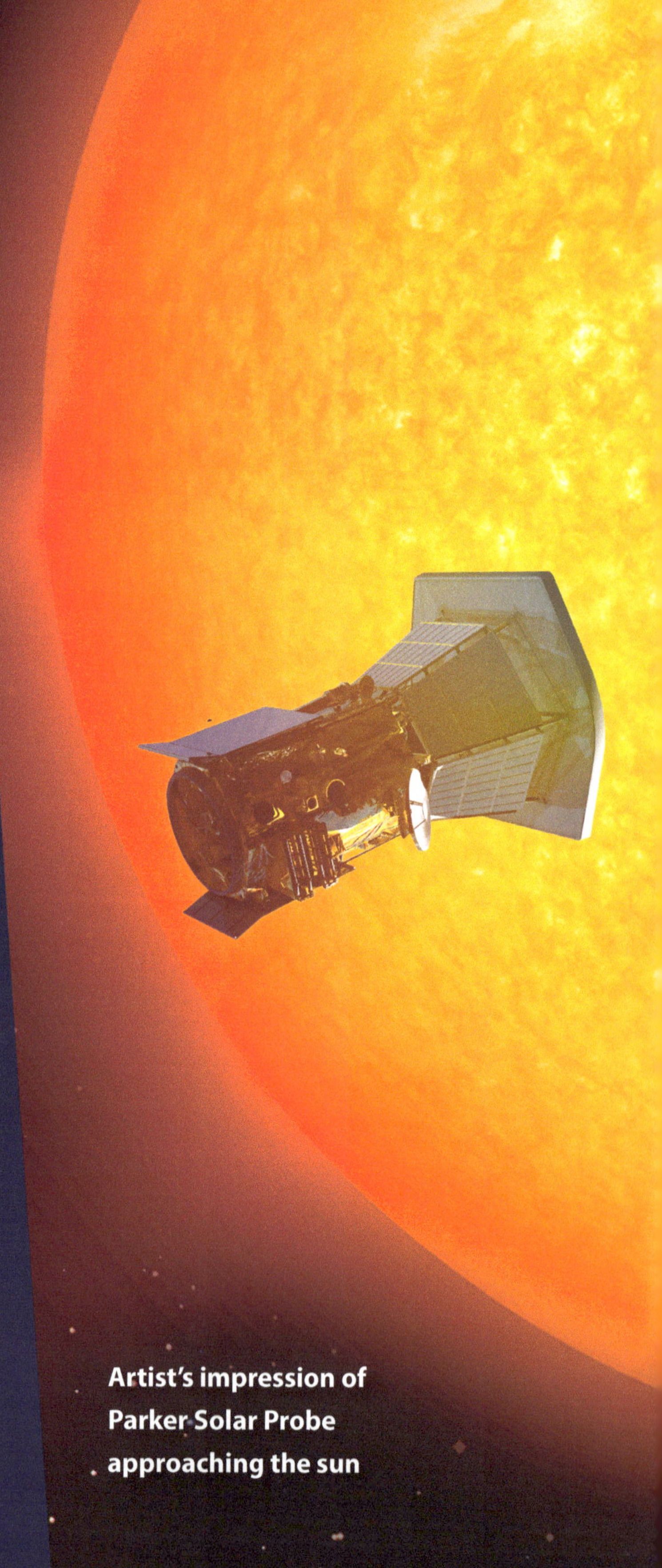

Artist's impression of Parker Solar Probe approaching the sun

Meet Bob Youngquist.

My dad worked on the Apollo missions, which carried astronauts to the surface of the moon. Now, I'm developing new technologies that will enable us to explore farther out in space—and possibly even touch the surface of the sun!

What is heat?

To protect a solar-surfing space **probe** from overheating, Youngquist will have to limit the flow of heat from the sun to the spacecraft. But just what is heat? And how does it flow from one thing to another?

All things are made up of tiny particles called **atoms.** These atoms are always moving and vibrating, even in solid matter. The motion gives every object internal energy, sometimes called **thermal energy** or *heat energy*. An object's thermal energy depends on how much its atoms are moving. If they are only moving a little, the object has a low level of thermal energy. If the atoms move a lot, the object has a high level of thermal energy.

Heat is a word that describes the flow of thermal energy. Heat is thermal energy that flows from a warmer object to a colder object. Any object that is warmer than its surroundings gives off heat. The sun gives off heat because it is much, much warmer than its surroundings. Even our bodies give off a little heat into their surroundings.

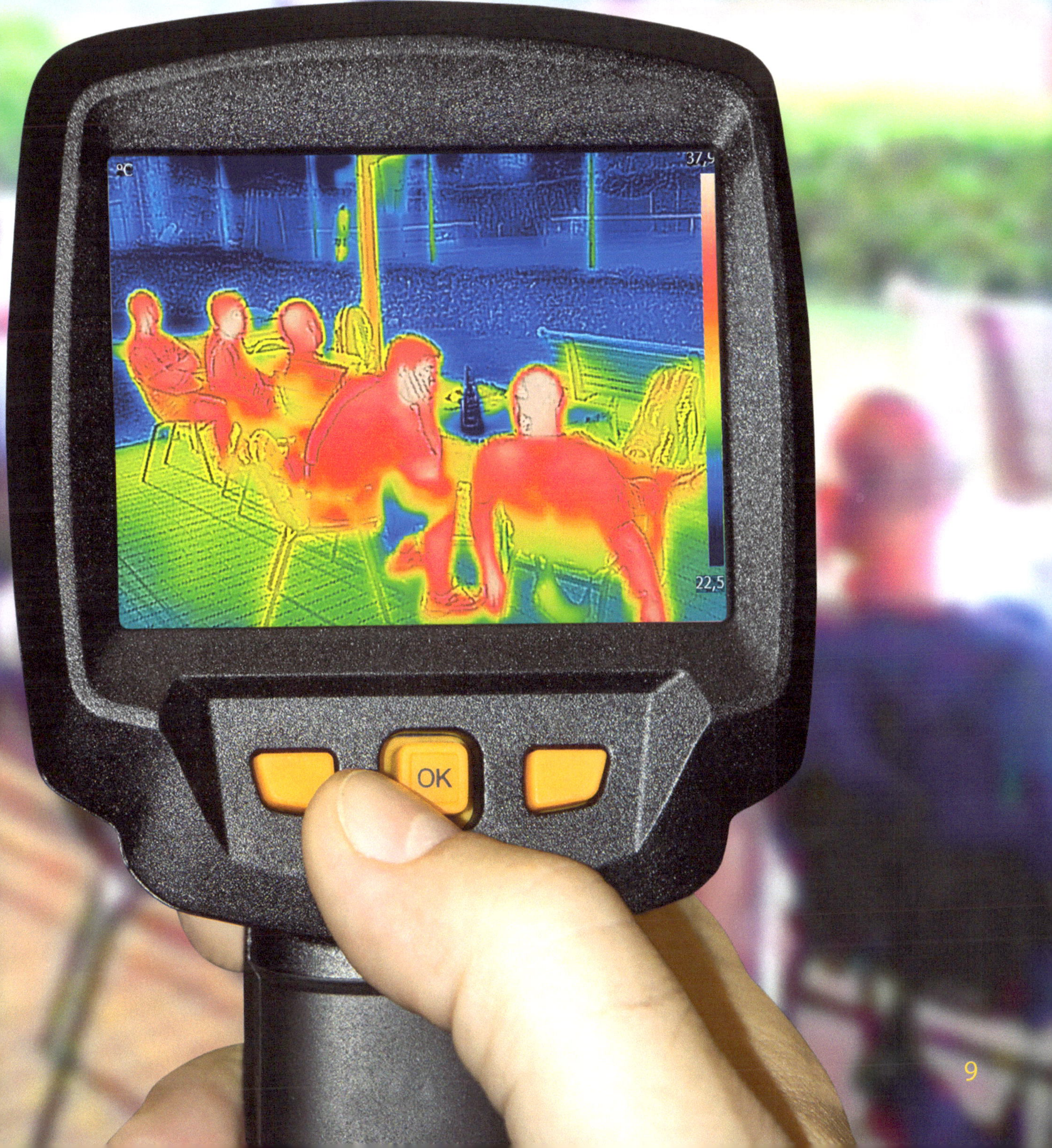

Everything emits heat—including people, as seen with this thermal camera.

How heat moves

Heat does not stay in one place. It naturally flows from warmer objects to cooler objects, in much the same way that water flows downhill.

" This transfer of heat occurs in three different ways: through **conduction, convection,** or **radiation.** " —Bob

Conduction is the spreading of heat through a material by collisions between **atoms.** Imagine a metal spoon placed in a hot pan. The pan transfers **thermal energy** to the atoms at the tip of the spoon, causing them to vibrate faster. These atoms strike neighboring atoms, causing them to move faster. In this way, thermal energy is

transferred, or conducted, along the spoon. The atoms themselves do not move through the spoon. Instead, they transfer heat from one to the next.

Convection is the transfer of heat by the movement of a liquid or gas. Picture a hot stove in a room. The stove warms the air around it. Warm air is less dense than cool air. So the warm air rises. As it rises, cool air rushes in to take its place. This air is in turn heated and rises as well. The rising of warm air and falling of cool air creates a pattern of movement called a *convection current,* spreading thermal energy throughout the room.

Outer space is nearly empty. There is no air or other fluid to transfer heat through **convection.** It is also extremely unlikely for a spacecraft to touch something, allowing the transfer of heat by **conduction.** So in space, heat is often transferred in a third way: **radiation.**

Radiation is energy given off in the form of waves or tiny particles of matter. Much of the sun's energy is given off in the form of **electromagnetic radiation.** The light we see is one form of electromagnetic radiation. But there are also many kinds of electromagnetic radiation invisible to our eyes.

Objects with lots of energy give off electromagnetic radiation in the form of tiny particles called **photons.** A photon travels from its source at a high speed. When a photon strikes an **atom,** the photon is either reflected or absorbed. If the atom absorbs the photon, it gains the photon's energy. Remember, objects whose atoms gain internal energy or **thermal energy** heat up. So by transferring energy, radiation transfers heat.

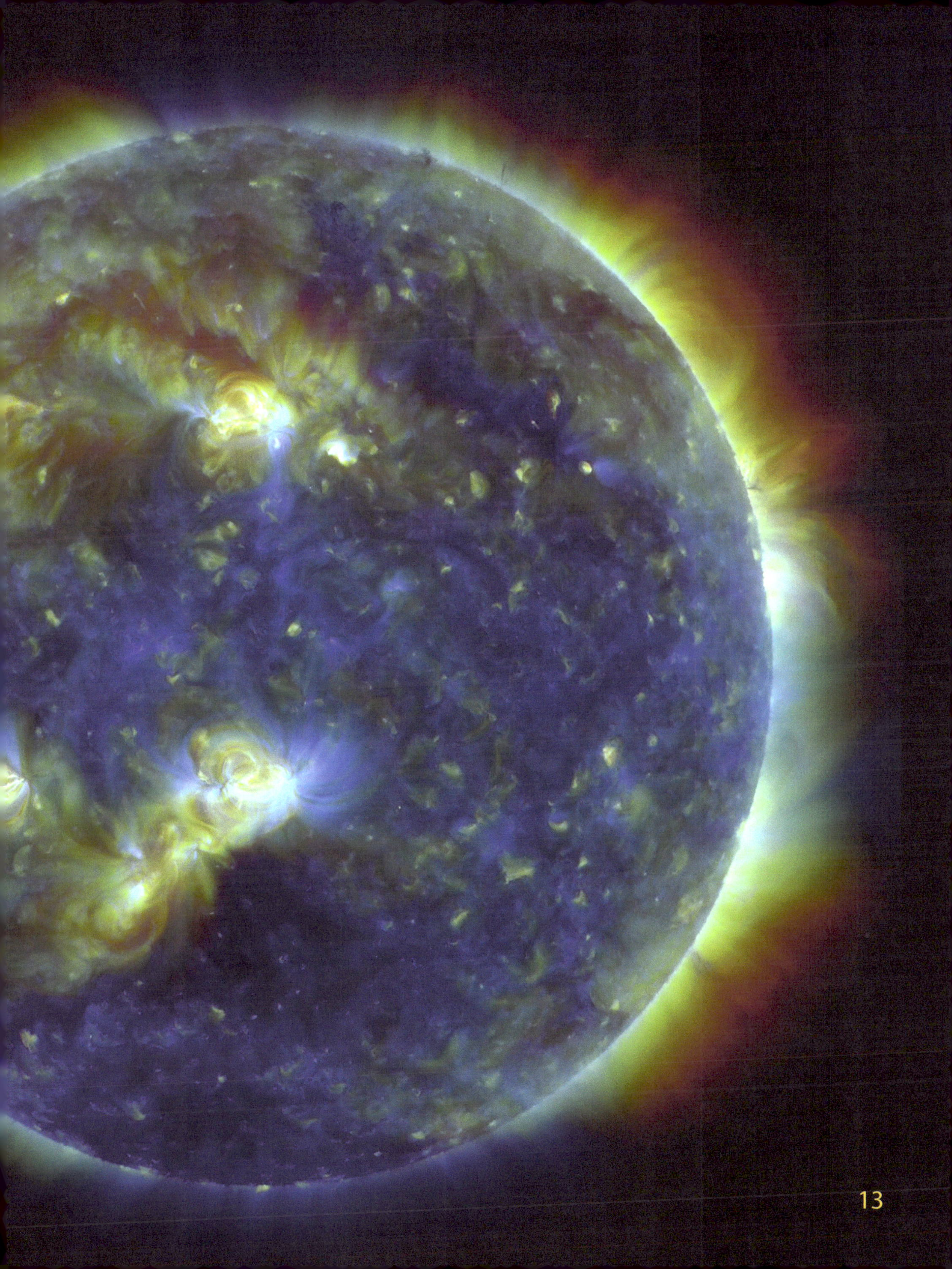

Youngquist was born in New York state. His family moved to the state of Florida when he was seven. Bob's father worked as an **engineer** for the manufacturer General Electric. Bob was inspired by his father's broad training and knowledge.

> **"** From rebuilding car transmissions to building houses, Dad seemed to do a little bit of everything. **"**
> —Bob

Lennart Youngquist

Bob was a self-proclaimed nerd. He loved the science-fiction television series "Star Trek" (1966-1969) and hung out with members of the chess club. Today, science and technology are an important part of pop culture, and many people proudly identify themselves as nerds. But in the 1960's and 1970's, the term *nerd* was a serious insult. To avoid bullies, Bob stuck close to his group of like-minded (nerdy) friends.

At General Electric, Bob's father worked on projects that contributed to NASA's Apollo program. And, living in Florida, Bob could watch rockets launched from Kennedy Space Center from his own backyard. Despite such close ties to the space program, Bob did not imagine pursuing a career in space technology himself.

❝ I wasn't really a space buff. ❞ —Bob

After briefly considering becoming a doctor, Bob returned to New York to get degrees in physics and mathematics from the University of Rochester. Then he went to Stanford University in California to get his Ph.D. degree in applied physics.

Absorbing and reflecting radiation

When a **photon** strikes a material, what happens next depends in part on the photon's energy level. Not all photons are created equal. A photon moves through space a bit like a wave. The distance from one *crest* (peak) of this wave to the next is called the photon's *wavelength,* and it is related to the photon's energy level. The higher the energy, the shorter the wavelength.

Some materials readily absorb photons of many energy levels or wavelengths. Others absorb photons of just a few energy levels, reflecting the rest. But all materials absorb at least some kinds of **radiation;** and all materials reflect at least some kinds, too.

With visible light, the *spectrum* (range) of wavelengths that an object absorbs and reflects gives the object its color. Imagine a bright red apple. Its surface absorbs most photons in the orange, yellow, green, blue, indigo, and violet regions of the visible spectrum. It reflects most photons in the red portion of the spectrum. It is these photons that are reflected to our eyes, causing us to see the color red.

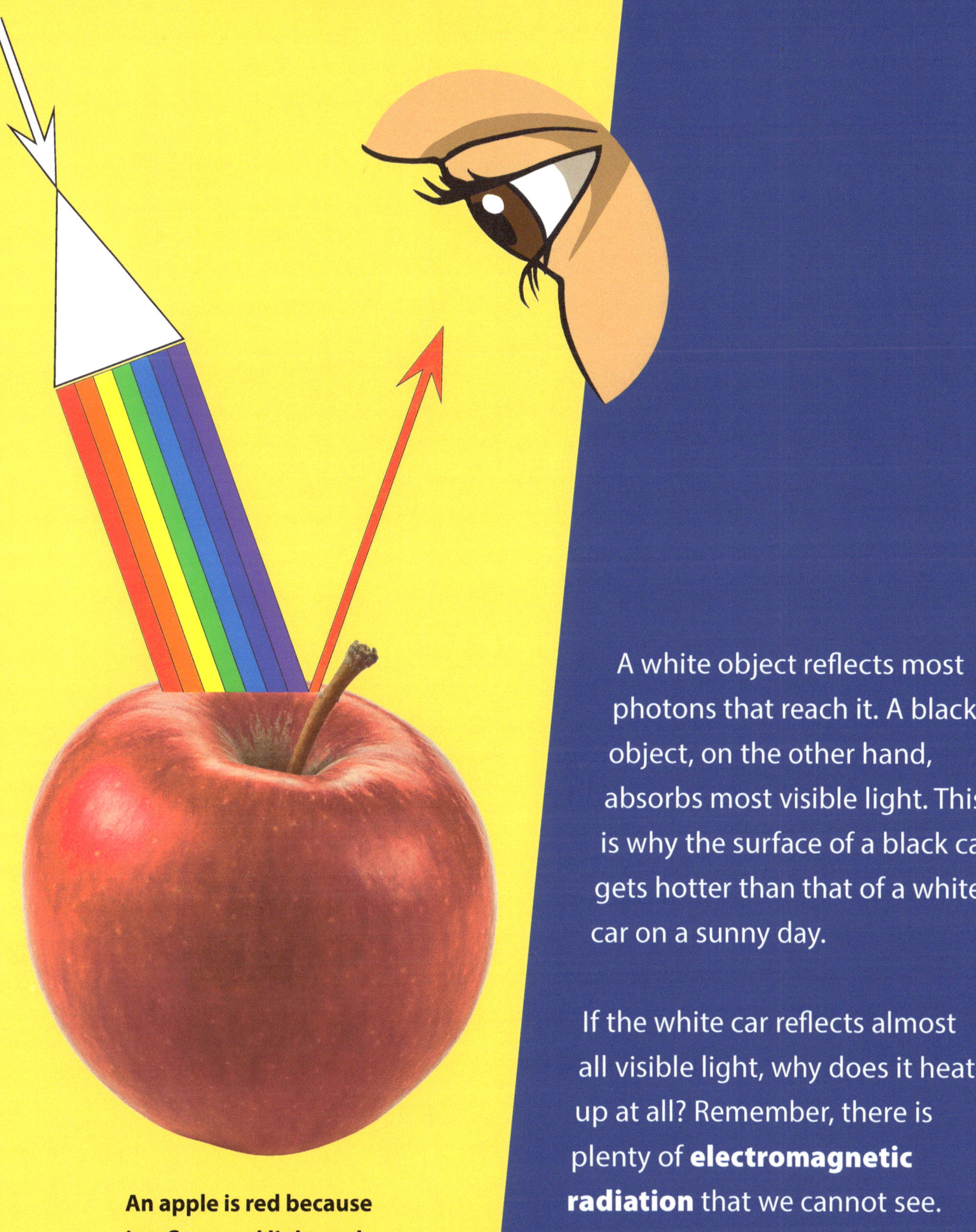

A white object reflects most photons that reach it. A black object, on the other hand, absorbs most visible light. This is why the surface of a black car gets hotter than that of a white car on a sunny day.

If the white car reflects almost all visible light, why does it heat up at all? Remember, there is plenty of **electromagnetic radiation** that we cannot see. The car absorbs some solar radiation invisible to our eyes.

An apple is red because it reflects red light and absorbs the other colors of the visible spectrum.

Energy from the sun

Any object that radiates heat gives off some **electromagnetic radiation.** However, the vast majority of electromagnetic radiation in our **solar system** is given off by the sun.

The sun's energy comes from nuclear fusion reactions deep inside the sun's core. The energy produced there is incredible, raising the core's temperature to over 15 million K. (One kelvin, K, is equal to one Celsius degree above absolute zero, −273.15 °C or −459.67 °F.) Tremendous **thermal energy** makes its way to the sun's surface, where it is radiated out into space.

The sun mostly emits visible light and *infrared rays,* which have slightly less energy than visible light. But the sun gives off small amounts of other forms of electromagnetic radiation, too, including radio waves, ultraviolet light, X rays, and gamma rays.

Earth catches a small fraction of this **radiation,** but it is enough to keep the surface a balmy 60 °F (15 °C) on average. The planet's huge **mass** and **convection** in the **atmosphere** help to absorb and distribute the sun's heat, keeping the planet at fa relatively steady temperature. But exposed to the extreme cold of space and intense radiation from the sun, a spacecraft can easily become far too hot or cold to work properly.

Lay out on the beach, and you'll feel the huge amount of heat that we get from the sun. — Bob

Practically all spacecraft have to take advantage of the ability to control how much radiation they absorb and how much they emit, in order to stay within whatever temperature range they want to be at. —Bob

Managing radiation

Spacecraft are not defenseless against the perils of solar **radiation.** There are ways to control radiative heat transfer to enable a craft to perform its mission.

The methods used to heat and cool spacecraft can be broken down into two types. They are **active thermal control** and **passive thermal control.**

Active thermal control involves the use of special devices, such as heaters and radiators, to keep a spacecraft within a desired temperature range. Such devices require power or some resource like coolant that gets used up over time.

Power and coolant are precious resources on a spacecraft. For this reason, mission planners tend to prefer passive thermal control. Passive control may involve the use of special coatings to limit the radiation taken in by a craft. It may also involve the use of special flight paths to limit or moderate the craft's exposure to sunlight.

After completing his Ph.D. degree in 1984, Youngquist had job offers from companies across the United States. Instead, he took a position teaching engineering at University College in London for two years. But Youngquist was putting in many hours doing scientific research on top of his teaching duties.

> I was heavily involved in optics [the study of light]; I was doing medical technology. —Bob

He was working too hard, and it took a toll on his health. Youngquist suffered from exhaustion. He returned to Florida to recover.

Around that time, space shuttle launches were resuming, after a long delay following the disastrous loss of the space shuttle Challenger in 1986. Kennedy Space Center was hiring **engineers.** As luck would have it, Bob's brother was working there in 1988 and referred him. Starting out as a contractor,

Bob opened a small lab that built optical tools to help maintain the **orbiters,** assemble space shuttles, and support launches. The lab eventually became NASA's Applied Physics Lab (APL).

1988 launch of space shuttle Discovery, the first flight after the Challenger disaster

Reflecting
solar energy

Special thermal coatings can be used to deflect solar energy, reducing the amount of heat taken on by a spacecraft. Such coatings are already widely used in space exploration. But current coatings are limited—they can reflect most, but not all, of the sun's **radiation.** The excess heat, however small, will build up over time, unless a craft has some sort of **active thermal control** device to cool it down.

The James Webb Space Telescope (JWST) provides a good example of the limits of thermal coatings. The JWST is an orbiting infrared telescope that will study distant planets and galaxies and peer back over 13 billion years into the universe's past.

Infrared telescopes must be kept at extremely cool temperatures to work properly. Earlier infrared space telescopes cooled themselves by venting a coolant into space. But the coolant gets used up over time, so such a space telescope can only be used for about a year. To make the JWST last longer, **engineers** designed it to use solar reflectors, instead of coolant. But current reflector technology can barely keep the instruments cold enough.

These reflectors must be folded up and packed for launch, and they must automatically unfold in space. Each layer is thinner

NASA engineers test the deployment of the JWST's delicate sunshade.

than the width of a human hair. In 2018, NASA reported that it had detected tears in the reflectors, setting back the JWST's launch.

Youngquist was studying ways to keep spacecraft cool when he stumbled upon an important piece of research. In 1961, the NASA scientist Robert R. Hibbard showed that it was possible to reach extremely cold temperatures in space, even in the presence of the sun, using reflectors. Furthermore, Hibbard suggested that such technology could be used to store rocket fuel (which has to be kept very cold) in space.

Convinced that he could improve upon current reflector technology and reach the cold temperatures needed, Youngquist applied for a grant from NIAC and was approved.

But I didn't understand the problems of the existing technology at the time. I thought that if I could just tweak the existing proposals, I could make this work. —Bob

Youngquist was following paths that had been unsuccessfully tried by others. He first experimented with traditional silvered mirrors. Such mirrors are panes of glass backed with silver or another metal—just like the mirrors in our homes. They reflect all the visible light that reaches them. But almost all metals absorb much ultraviolet **radiation.** In testing, a mirrored sphere cooled down to about 155 K (-118 °C or −181 °F)—pretty chilly, but not cold enough for Youngquist's needs.

Youngquist then turned to *dielectric mirrors.* Dielectric mirrors are mirrors covered with extremely thin films of materials that can filter out certain wavelengths of light. But to even test such materials would have cost many tens of thousands of dollars—more than Youngquist could afford.

Unable to find a solution, Youngquist was about to return his grant money to NIAC. But then he came up with an idea. He thought of the ceramic tiles that cover the space shuttle.

Space shuttle tile

Tiles from the shuttle

The space shuttle program was a United States human space flight system. It made use of partly reusable vehicles that could land much like ordinary airplanes. The airplane-like part of the space shuttle, which carried the crew and cargo, was called the **orbiter.** At take-off, the shuttle also included two reusable rocket engines and one large disposable fuel tank. These pieces separated from the orbiter in the first few minutes of flight, falling back toward Earth. Space shuttles flew from 1981 to 2011.

Reusing the space shuttle orbiter posed special challenges. **Engineers** had to choose materials that could protect the orbiter from the extreme cold of space and the extreme heat of reentering Earth's **atmosphere.** The materials had to be *modular* (made up of smaller pieces) and replaceable, so damaged parts could be easily swapped out. The materials also had to be lightweight and easy to manufacture.

NASA chose several different materials to coat different parts of the orbiter. But the most common material was specialized ceramic tiles, covering more than half of each orbiter.

> **"** People have actually talked to me about using them as **laser** shields. I thought, 'Wait a minute! If these things can be used as laser shields, they surely can reflect sunlight!' **"** —Bob

Youngquist thought that these space shuttle tiles could be the key to developing a better solar reflector. They already resisted heat well, and they were pretty easy to make.

If space shuttle tiles resist heat so well, why can't engineers just use them to keep spacecraft cool? The tiles are made of glass. Glass does not absorb much ultraviolet or visible radiation. But glass does absorb infrared waves—which makes up almost half of the sun's radiation output. So although the approach was promising, a different material was needed.

Big idea:
Solar White

Youngquist was able to identify several materials that would reflect all the **electromagnetic radiation** the sun emits—not just visible light—and would be able to withstand the process of being baked into a ceramic tile.

Think about snow, salt, and sugar. These things are made of tiny grains that are *transparent* (clear) by themselves. But together, they appear white. This is because most of the visible light that strikes them is deflected or reflected back out. A tile of Youngquist's material—which he calls Solar White—works in much the same way. A coating of transparent particles

Down to Earth:

Ideas from space that could serve us on our planet.

scatters and deflects solar **radiation** striking the tile, preventing the material from absorbing heat.

Remember that silvered mirrors absorb too much ultraviolet radiation to be of use in space. That's true of traditional mirrors, but a silver backing to a Solar White tile helps to reflect the last bit of infrared and visible light back out into space. The scattering material reflects almost all the ultraviolet light before it reaches the silvering.

Solar White is specifically designed to work in space. But coatings that can scatter electromagnetic radiation have uses here on the ground, too. For example, some cities require new roofs to be as bright as possible to reflect the sun's rays, helping to alleviate the heat that collects in urban areas. In warm climates, reflective roof surfaces can help keep a building's interior cooler.

New York City has painted about 7 million square feet of tar rooftops white to lower temperatures.

Testing
Solar White

> **"** One of the key challenges is testing this material. How do we know it works? **"** —Bob

The **radiation** present at Earth's surface is not pure sunlight. Earth's **atmosphere** filters out much of the sun's radiation. Furthermore, everything on Earth emits heat energy in the form of infrared radiation.

To determine how Solar White would perform in space, Youngquist and his team put each sample through a rigorous testing process. They put the sample in a black chamber. They pumped all the air out of the chamber and chilled it to about 30 K (–243 °C or –406 °F). Then, they shone a special kind of lamp called a xenon arc lamp on the sample.

A few different compounds have performed well in this test. But the testing process is not perfect.

Youngquist is working to develop a CubeSat to test Solar White directly. A CubeSat is a small satellite—usually about

Caption: Laboratory testing of Solar White

> **"** A xenon arc lamp matches up pretty well, but it doesn't have the same ultraviolet signature that the sun has. **"** —Bob

the size of a loaf of bread—that can be launched into space along with other CubeSats or larger spacecraft. The CubeSat will expose the material to the sun and evaluate its performance. With a CubeSat test, Youngquist hopes to convince scientists and **engineers** to start using Solar White in their spacecraft missions.

Youngquist heads the Applied Physics Lab at NASA's Kennedy Space Center in Florida. He uses his background in math and physics to help his team to solve problems.

> All kinds of problems emerge here at Kennedy that we have to step in and deal with. They can range from figuring out how to get vultures away from the launch pad to developing high-end new technology for **sensors.** —Bob

Youngquist was no stranger to the space shuttle **orbiter** tiles when he came up with his idea for Solar White. One of the problems he solved at the APL was how to remove water from the tiles.

Orbiter tiles are extremely *porous* (filled with tiny holes), like a sponge. Before space shuttle launches, the tiles were filled with a waterproofing material to keep moisture out of them. But this material burned away as the craft reentered Earth's **atmosphere,** leaving the tiles vulnerable to rain. An orbiter with waterlogged tiles was too heavy to launch again. Youngquist discovered that water could be vacuumed out of the tiles through the same hole used to fill them with the waterproofing material. This method shaved months off the process of drying out a shuttle orbiter.

Bob with his wife Sharon in front of an orbiter and carrier airplane

Surfing the sun

The sun is the center of our **solar system** and the source of energy for almost all forms of life on Earth. But some things about it still puzzle scientists. For example, the sun is only about 5800 K at its surface. But the outer layer of the sun's **atmosphere,** called the *corona,* can reach millions of kelvins. Astronomers are not sure why this is the case.

The Parker Solar Probe will fly to within 3.9 million miles (6.2 million kilometers) of the sun's surface, close enough to enter the corona. The **probe** has four instruments designed to study the sun's electric and **magnetic fields** and the energetic particles given off by the sun, known as the solar wind. The Parker Solar Probe will experience temperatures of up to 1670 K at the point in its **orbit** closest to the sun. But it will travel in a highly elongated orbit to limit its solar exposure, flying past the orbit of Venus at its farthest point.

Coated with Solar White, a probe could possibly get all the way to the surface of the sun. There, it could examine the area in which the gases in the corona heat up and expand. This would help scientists understand the strange temperature difference between the sun's surface and its corona. Doug Willard, a colleague of Youngquist at Kennedy Space Center, is working to develop such a solar-surfing probe with another NIAC grant.

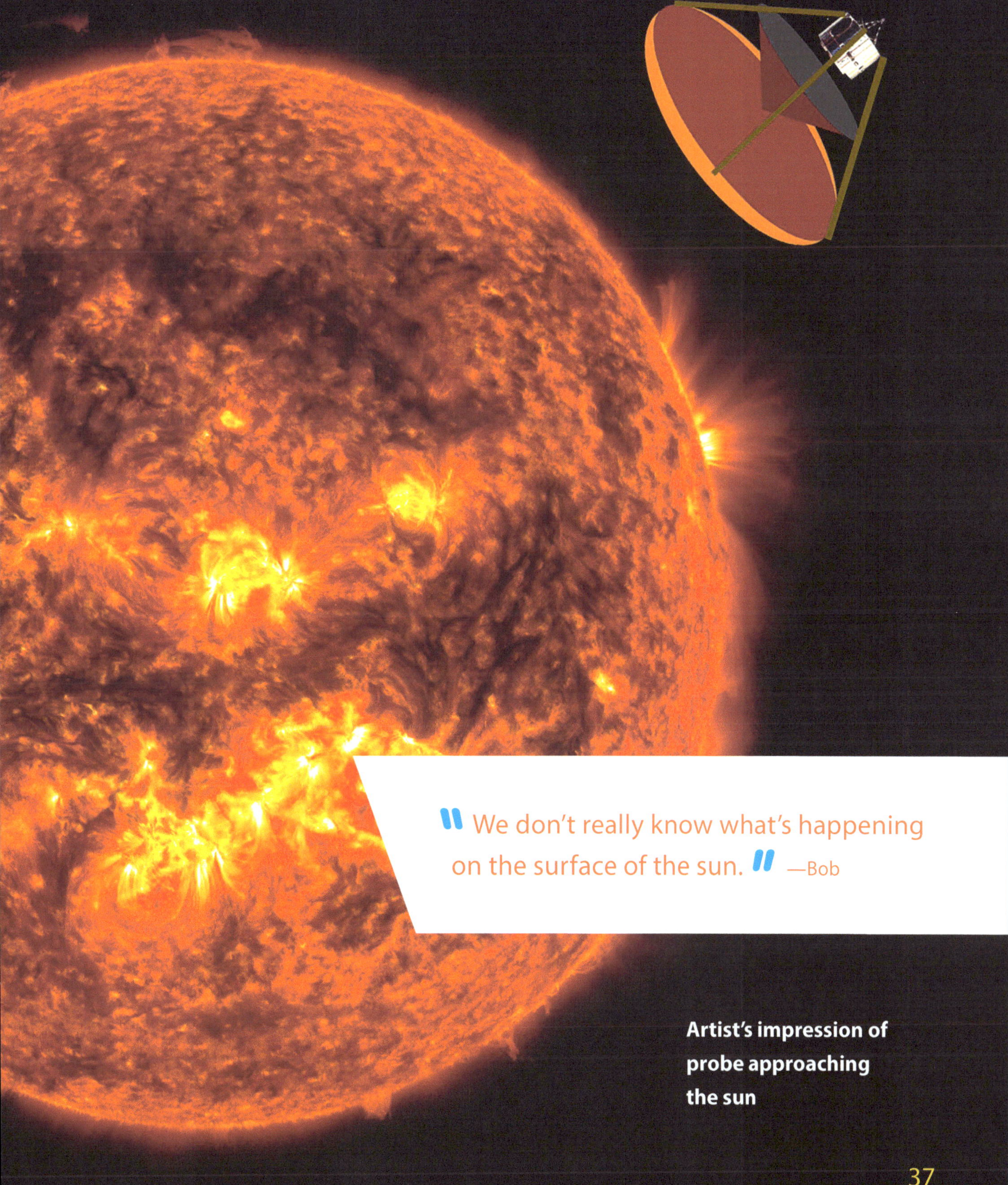

Artist's impression of probe approaching the sun

Other uses

Thermal control is a problem for all spacecraft, not just those that study the sun. Solar White could make possible a whole host of new space applications.

Fill 'er up!

Imagine there were no gas stations, and you could only refuel your automobile at home. Every time you left the house, you'd need to fill the tank with enough gasoline for the entire journey. And don't forget to bring enough fuel to make it back home! If you were planning a long trip, you might need to trade in your car for a tanker truck.

Rockets face this problem all the time. They need **propellant** to get spacecraft to different destinations. Right now, the rockets must carry all their propellant with them. And propellant is heavy—it takes even more propellant to lift all that propellant into space.

For years, mission planners have dreamed of storing propellant in space—essentially creating outer space refueling stations. But most propellant is stored in liquid form. It must be kept extremely cold or it will evaporate into a gas. A cooling technology like Solar White could help **engineers** set up filling stations in **orbit,** on the moon, or on **asteroids,** enabling the rockets of the future to gas up and go!

To the stars

There's a big group at NASA that would like to launch **interstellar probes.** They would like to launch probes that would go so fast that they would leave the **solar system** and fly right past Pioneer and Voyager, the probes that are farthest out there. The only way they know to achieve that kind of speed is to slingshot around the sun. —Bob

Distances in outer space are pretty mind-blowing. To get around more quickly, spacecraft can use a trick called the Oberth maneuver (named for the German rocket pioneer Hermann Oberth). In the Oberth maneuver, a spacecraft flies close to a massive object, such as a planet. Firing its engines at closest approach gives the craft a boost of speed as it goes flinging away again. In effect, the craft takes advantage of the object's gravitational pull to slingshot itself to a higher speed.

Nothing in our solar system is more massive than the sun, and nothing has a stronger gravitational pull. A Solar White-coated spacecraft might get close enough to the sun to slingshot away at incredible speeds, reaching distant stars in a matter of decades, rather than centuries.

Protecting astronauts

Youngquist actually began his quest to develop Solar White while trying to tackle another challenge of space travel. Remember that **electromagnetic radiation** is only one kind of **radiation.** Radiation can also be given off in the form of particles. Earth's **magnetic field** deflects almost all this particle radiation. But in outer space, **particle radiation** can be dangerous or deadly to astronauts.

Youngquist explored the idea of generating magnetic fields around spacecraft, protecting astronauts in much the same way that Earth's magnetic field protects us. But the electronics required to generate such a field only function at extremely low temperatures. The need to keep such electronics cool put Youngquist on the path to developing Solar White.

This illustration
shows Earth's
magnetosphere
(blue) in the solar
wind (not to scale).

Robert Youngquist and the Applied Physics Lab

From left to right: Thomas Moss, Teresa Lawhorn, Stanley Starr, Ellen Arens, Bob Youngquist, Curtis Ihlefeld, Janine Captain, Mark Nurge

Glossary

active thermal control controlling the thermal energy of a spacecraft through the use of devices, such as heaters or radiators.

asteroid a rocky or metallic body smaller than a planet that orbits the sun.

atmosphere the mass of gases that surrounds a planet or other body in space.

atom one of the most basic units of matter, consisting of a *nucleus* (core) of particles called *protons* and *neutrons* with tiny particles called *electrons* moving around the nucleus.

conduction the transfer of heat by collisions between neighboring atoms.

convection the transfer of heat by the movement of a liquid or gas.

element a basic unit of matter that contains only one kind of atom.

engineer a person who uses scientific principles to design structures, such as bridges and skyscrapers, machines, and all sorts of products.

electromagnetic radiation energy given off in the form of *oscillating* (moving back and forth) electric and magnetic fields. Visible light, infrared rays, ultraviolet light and X rays are all kinds of electromagnetic radiation.

fusion the combining of two atomic nuclei to form the nucleus of a heavier *element* (a basic unit of matter that contains only one kind of atom).

interstellar between the stars.

laser a device that produces a very powerful beam of light.

magnetic field the invisible area of magnetic influence, or effect, surrounding a magnet or magnetic objects.

mass the amount of matter something contains.

orbit a looping path around an object in space; the condition of circling a massive object in space under the influence of the object's gravity.

orbiter a spacecraft designed to orbit a planet or other object in space; usually refers to the airplane-like part of the U.S. space shuttle that carried crew and cargo.

particle radiation energy given off in the form of high-speed *subatomic* (smaller than an atom) particles.

passive thermal control controlling the thermal energy of a spacecraft without the use of devices, for example by altering its flight path or coating it with reflective materials.

photon a tiny particle of electromagnetic radiation.

probe a rocket, satellite, or other unmanned spacecraft carrying scientific instruments, to record or report back information about space.

propellant solid or liquid fuel that is turned into gas and put under pressure to push a spacecraft forward.

radiation energy given off in the form of waves or tiny particles of matter.

sensor a device that detects heat, light, or some other phenomenon, producing an electrical signal.

solar system the sun and everything that travels around it, including Earth and all the other planets and their moons.

thermal energy the energy an object has because of the movement of its atoms; internal energy.

Inventor challenge:
Space refueling depot

Bob Youngquist's Solar White coating will make it possible to store rocket fuel in space for long durations. Your challenge is to design the first refueling depot in space.

STEP 1 — Think about the challenge

The kinds of missions that would need refueling haven't been developed yet, so your first task is to think about those potential missions. Would this refueling depot be used by astronauts—or even tourists or colonists—traveling to Mars? Would it help send large robotic rovers to the far reaches of the solar system? Or would it refuel small probes with huge engines to propel them to other star systems? The types of missions you expect the depot to serve will influence its location. Will it be in orbit around Earth? At a Lagrange point? On Mars's moon Phobos? Somewhere else?

STEP 2 — Create your prototype

Draw up your depot prototype, taking its construction and use into account. Will it be constructed in multiple pieces like the International Space Station? Will tankers replenish its fuel, or will it make its own? Will it have a crew, or will it be completely autonomous? Research how spacecraft travel through the solar system to inform your design, especially how they use the gravitational pull of planets and other bodies.

STEP 3 — Share your design

Share your design with friends, classmates, or teachers. Explain the different design possibilities and why you chose your design. Do they agree or disagree with your choices? If possible, share your design with engineers and scientists and ask for their input.

STEP 4 — Grow your idea

See if anyone you shared your idea with will design missions that will use your refueling depot. Revise your refueling depot to accommodate their missions, if necessary. Together, you can design the next steps in space exploration!

Index